HISTORY'S
VILLAINS

FRANCISCO
PIZARRO

Scott Ingram

BLACKBIRCH®
PRESS

THOMSON
™
GALE

San Diego • Detroit • New York • San Francisco • Cleveland
New Haven, Conn. • Waterville, Maine • London • Munich

Photo credits: Cover, pages 20, 51, 70, 75, 82, 96 © North Wind Archives; pages 5, 26, 33, 42, 49, 60,
90 © historypictures.com; pages 8, 16, 29, 56, 66, 99 © Bettmann/CORBIS; page 18: Archiving Early
America; page 37 © Archivo Iconografico, S.A./CORBIS; page 79 © Galen Rowell/CORBIS

LIBRARY OF CONGRESS CATALOGING-IN-PUBLICATION DATA

Ingram, Scott
  Francisco Pizarro / by Scott Ingram.
    p. cm. — (History's villains series)
Includes index.
  ISBN 1-56711-627-2 (hardback : alk. paper)
  1. Pizarro, Francisco, ca. 1475-1541—Juvenile literature. 2. Peru—History—Conquest,
1522-1548—Juvenile literature. 3. Incas—Juvenile literature. 4. Indians, Treatment of-
South America—History—Juvenile literature. 5. Conquerors—Peru—Biography—Juvenile
literature. 6. Conquerors—Spain—Biography—Juvenile literature. I. Title. II.
History's villains.
  F3442.P776 I64 2003
  985'.02'092—dc21   2002004577

Printed in United States
10 9 8 7 6 5 4 3 2 1

CONTENTS

INTRODUCTION: "WHY DOESN'T THE BOOK SAY ANYTHING?"

The Spanish soldiers were in position for a surprise attack. Swords drawn, guns and crossbows loaded, horses reined tight, they awaited the result of the meeting between Father Vincent de Valverde and the Inca king.

The commander of the Spanish, Captain Francisco Pizarro, had ordered Valverde, a Catholic priest, to stand in the central plaza of Cajamarca, an Inca city in present-day Peru. While Pizarro hid with his men, the priest went forward to greet the Inca ruler, Atahualpa. Once the king, his nobles, and his personal guards were in the square, Valverde was to explain to the king that the Spaniards were there to bring Christianity to the Inca. Any resistance from the Inca would be met with deadly force.

The Spaniards had arrived several days before and found Cajamarca deserted. Atahualpa had ordered the residents to leave. As Pizarro's men waited in alleyways surrounding the public square, they were eager to spring into action. The sooner the Incas were defeated, the faster they themselves could take the Incas' gold and silver. There was more than enough for anyone—more than any white person had ever seen. Over the course of their march though Inca lands, the Spaniards had seen goblets, plates, masks, jewelry, statues, and countless other objects made of precious metal and rare gems. Only among the Aztec of Mexico was there wealth like this, the Spaniards agreed. Yet much of

Atahualpa was a fierce ruler who demanded respect.

that wealth was already in the hands of the Spanish nobles. The Inca wealth was almost untouched.

At last, the Inca king and his party approached the walled city of Cajamarca. First to enter the square were guards dressed in red and black tunics of fine alpaca wool. Next slaves came who swept the street in front of the king as he approached. A large group of nobles on foot walked on the cleaned ground, with their crowns of gold and silver that shone brightly. Finally, Atahualpa came into view, seated high on a gold-plated litter carried by a dozen men. The Inca ruler wore a headdress with brilliant feathers from tropical birds. Surrounded by guards, the king was carried forward to meet the priest.

Valverde spoke first. He said that he brought greetings from a king across the ocean. Then he read a document that claimed the ownership of Peru for the Spanish king. He went on to say "I am a priest of God, and I teach Christians the things of God, and in like manner I come to teach you."

Valverde demanded that the Inca ruler and his subjects turn away from their beliefs and submit to Christianity. Atahualpa, who was worshiped as a god by his people, demanded to know who gave Valverde the authority to tell the Incas what to do. The priest held up his Bible and said, "What I teach is that which God says to us in this Book."

"Give me the book so it can speak to me," Atahualpa said. He took the Bible from the priest and held it to his ear as if listening to hear its commands. Then, he threw the Bible to the ground and asked, "Why doesn't the book say anything to me?"

Valverde turned away from the Inca king's insult. He walked away from the square as Pizarro stepped into view. The Spanish commander waved a white handkerchief, a signal to attack. Suddenly, guns roared and trumpeters blew the call to charge. Clouds of crossbow darts whirred across the square. Foot soldiers and cavalrymen charged from alleys and doorways into the mass of Incas.

Most of the Incas, who had never seen horses before, fled in panic, and stumbled over one another as they tried to escape. The Spanish horsemen trampled and slashed at the Incas as they rode among them. Meanwhile, the foot soldiers, with razor-sharp steel swords and axes, killed with a fury. In minutes, hundreds of Incas lay dead in the square.

Amid the slaughter, Pizarro ran toward the Inca ruler, but he did not join in the killing. Instead, he grabbed Atahualpa by the arm and pulled him to safety as the Spaniards killed the litter-bearers. Pizarro's gesture was not made out of respect or concern for Atahualpa. Pizarro knew that he could gain power over the Inca empire if he held its king as a prisoner. Atahualpa's gold-threaded clothing had been torn off by greedy Spanish soldiers. He was chained and taken to a room that overlooked the square in which thousands of his people now lay dead.

That day of slaughter in November 1532 put Pizarro firmly in control of one of the largest empires in the world at that time. By then, the Inca empire was already weakened by civil war and by European diseases. Pizarro proceeded to remove tons of gold in a few short years, while he oversaw the extermination of a people and a culture. Within 10 years, a kingdom of 12 million people was only a memory.

CHAPTER 1

DEATH, FAITH, AND A NEW WORLD

$\mathcal{M}$ore than 500 years after Christopher Columbus first set foot in the Bahamas, the European conquest of the Americas remains one of the most important eras in Western history. The era began in the newly united nation of Spain during a time of famine, disease, and religious persecution. It continued with the discovery of a land that was unknown among Europeans.

It ended when, within 50 years of the European discovery of the New World, two mighty Native American empires lay in ruins.

Opposite: During the Spanish Inquisition thousands of people were burned at the stake.

Millions of Native Americans were dead from war and disease. The vast wealth of the Aztecs and the Incas was under the control of brutal Spanish soldiers and their royal employers.

The early European explorers were men who became as well known for their cruelty as for their daring and perseverance. Those who led Spanish expeditions—Cortés, Balboa, de Soto—are largely remembered as greedy and ruthless men. Among these men, one stands out for his determination, his treachery, and utter lack of concern for the lives of the Native Americans. He was Francisco Pizarro, the man who destroyed the Inca empire.

Death an Everyday Event

Francisco Pizarro was born in the town of Trujillo, Spain, in about 1471. His father, Gonzalo Pizarro, was an officer in the army of the Spanish province of Castille, who was not married to Francisco's mother, Francisca Gonzalez. Francisca later had four other sons who were Francisco's half brothers.

Francisco spent his childhood tending pigs on his grandparents' farm. His mother and his grandparents were peasants who had no opportunity for education, and as Francisco grew up, he never learned to read or write. He remained illiterate for his entire life, which was not unusual at that time.

Pizarro also grew up at time in which early death was a common daily event. Throughout much of the 15th century, famine gripped the countryside in the Spanish states of Andalusia, Castille, and Pizarro's native state, Estremadura. Starvation was not unusual among peasants such as those who worked the land. Most crops and livestock went as payment of taxes to the nobility who lived lives of great wealth and privilege.

Famine was not the only common cause of death in Pizarro's time. In the 1400s, the bubonic plague—known as the Black Death—passed through Spain four separate times and killed more than 125,000 people. Other diseases, such as cholera, smallpox, measles, and typhoid fever, frequently broke out and killed thousands in a matter of weeks.

Death also came in the form of religious violence. Pizarro's childhood and early adult years took place during one of the most terrifying periods in religious history, a time that influenced the lives of people both rich and poor. This era, known as the Spanish Inquisition, began while the nation of Spain itself was being formed.

A Land of Many Cultures

Once part of the Roman Empire, the country that became Spain was populated for centuries by a wide range of cultures and faiths. Many of the earliest settlers were Christian peoples from Europe. Because the land, called the Iberian Peninsula, was directly across the Strait of Gibraltar, it also drew people from North Africa. Those people, followers of the Islamic religion, migrated to Iberia in the eighth and ninth centuries. During that time, Jews also settled in the peninsula after they were driven out of the Middle East, North Africa, and southern Europe.

Throughout the 10th and 11th centuries, this mix of cultures and faiths on the Iberian Peninsula was ruled by Arab kings from North Africa known as the Moors. The Moorish empire was composed of nation states in which science, art, and culture flourished.

By the 12th and 13th centuries, Christian—or Catholic—states, led by the army of the state of Castille, had begun to drive the Moorish rulers off the peninsula. The Castillians began a *reconquista*—reconquest—of the region for the Catholic faith. This *reconquista* continued throughout much of the 1400s.

The birth of the nation that became Spain began in 1469, when Isabella, heir to the throne of Castille, married Ferdinand, heir to the throne of Aragon. This union brought together the two most powerful states on the peninsula. These states had risen to power through different methods.

Castille, a landlocked state, was a military power led by a nobility that followed a strict version of Catholicism. The Castillians believed in the forceful conversion of all non-Catholics to their faith—people who did not convert were tortured and burned alive. Castille's economic power came largely from taking the riches of non-Catholic states that its army conquered.

Aragon, by contrast, was a state in which the largest city was the Mediterranean Sea port of Barcelona. It had become wealthy through the establishment of trade relations across the Mediterranean, especially with Genoa, an Italian city-state. Aragon's economic power was based on trade and on the establishment of trading outposts in the Mediterranean region.

The union of the two most powerful states on the Iberian Peninsula began a series of conflicts that lasted several decades as Castille and Aragon brought other states under their control. In 1478, Queen Isabella, who hoped to unify her nation, made a decision that had a far-reaching effect. A Catholic like her Castillian ancestors, she felt that her nation could never be united unless its people all followed—or were converted to—the faith in which she believed.

Isabella called upon her political and religious advisor, Father Tomás de Torquemada, to begin an inquiry of all Spain's people to determine the sincerity of their faith. This inquiry, or inquisition, was aimed mainly at two groups, Jews and *conversos*—those who had converted to Catholicism from another faith. The Spanish Inquisition was more than simply a series of questions about one's religious beliefs. It was instead an ordeal of brutality, torture, and death.

Those whom the Inquisition determined to be insincere Catholics—as well as Jews, Muslims, and any other people who would not convert—were tortured and burned at the stake. Mercy was shown only to those who converted to Catholicism before they were burned. They were strangled to death before the flames consumed them, to spare them horrible pain. During the Spanish Inquisition, thousands of men, women, and children suffered agonizing tortures and gruesome deaths in every corner of the Iberian Peninsula.

Against this backdrop of famine, disease, and the Inquisition, Pizarro grew to adulthood and, as his father had done, joined the military. In 1492, when he was about 21, two key events took place that affected the history of Western civilization and changed the course of Pizarro's life.

In January 1492, Granada, the last Moorish state, fell to the combined armies of Castille and Aragon. Followers of Islam were banished from the kingdom. Ferdinand and Isabella had finally established a united nation of Spain. In March of that year, Isabella's first public proclamation as queen of Spain was to expel all Jews from the country. Any Jews who remained after July 1, the queen declared, would be burned alive. That date was later extended to August 2. With that expulsion, Isabella believed, Spain would at last be a unified Catholic nation.

At about that same time, an Italian sailor from Genoa appeared before the Spanish court. His name was Christopher Columbus, and he had approached rulers across Europe to seek financial support for a voyage to Asia. Columbus believed he could reach the Far East if he sailed west. It was a shorter route, he claimed, than to sail south around the continent of Africa and across the Indian Ocean, as explorers up to that time had done.

In April 1492, shortly after they signed the order to expel the Jews, Ferdinand and Isabella agreed to fund an expedition by Columbus. The king and queen had

15

Christopher Columbus visited the court of Ferdinand and Isabella in hopes of gaining their support for his voyage.

different reasons for their support of the expedition. Isabella wanted to carry the spirit of the *reconquista* to nonbelievers. With the Spanish treasury no longer drained by internal conflict, she was eager to support a voyage to spread her Catholicism. Ferdinand, true to his roots in Aragon's commercial economy, saw the voyage as an opportunity to establish trading outposts in foreign lands. The spices, silks, and jewels of Asia drew his interest, and he believed that an investment in Columbus would pay off handsomely.

Columbus set off on his voyage on August 1, 1492. Historians believe that some members of his crew were Jews or *conversos* who fled the Inquisition. By October, the men on Columbus's ships—the *Niña, Pinta*, and *Santa Maria*—had landed on a tropical island and claimed it for Spain. They were greeted by natives that Columbus called Indians after the land he believed he had reached—India. In truth, he had landed on San Salvador, an island in the Bahamas off the coast of present-day Florida.

Disappointment and Revolt

Little is known of Pizarro's life during the last decade of the 15th century. As a member of the royal army, he may have participated in a series of brief wars with Italian city-states that broke out during that time.

While Pizarro learned the art of war, the Spaniards under Columbus, who thought they had traveled to India, came to understand that they had discovered instead an enormous new land that did not exist on the maps in Europe. After his initial landing, Christopher

17

Columbus believed he had landed in India when he reached land in October 1492.

Columbus continued to sail farther into the Caribbean Sea. He landed on the island of Cuba and on Hispaniola—which holds the modern-day countries of Haiti and the Dominican Republic—and claimed both for Spain.

After he established a small settlement on Hispaniola, Columbus returned to Spain in January 1493. Still convinced that he had found a route to Asia, Columbus insisted to the king and queen that the island of Cuba was really the island of Japan.

Ferdinand and Isabella immediately made arrangements to send a much larger expedition back to the lands Columbus had claimed. A fleet of 17 ships that could carry 1,500 men was assembled for the voyage. Columbus was given orders to convert the Indians, expand his settlement on Hispaniola, and establish trading centers.

As those preparations were made, Isabella used her influence with Pope Alexander, the leader of the Catholic Church, which was based in Rome. She requested that the church give its approval to Spain's claims to the lands Columbus had discovered. The pope agreed to the queen's request and issued a decree in 1493, which granted Spain ownership of all "distant lands to the west."

Columbus arrived at Hispaniola with the large fleet in November 1493. He found that the settlement he had left behind less than a year earlier had been destroyed and all its inhabitants killed. The natives had revolted against the Spanish claim of ownership to their land, as well as to the Spaniards' violent efforts to colonize and convert them.

19

Spanish conquistadors
wanted to spread the
Catholic faith and gain
riches for themselves.

Columbus now found himself caught between two different visions of the Spanish presence in the New World. As a native of Genoa, he was more a merchant than a military or religious leader. In his view, the purpose of his voyages was to establish commerce and trading centers for the Spanish crown. This would enable him to repay the crown's investment and gain wealth for himself. The discovery of the ransacked settlement, however, changed the goal of many people in Columbus's party from one of peaceful trade to one of military expansion and forceful religious conversion. The old idea of the *reconquista* evolved into a new idea of conquest.

Soon, Spaniards who ventured into the New World became known as conquistadors—conquerors. Among the first conquistadors was a career soldier who arrived in Hispaniola in 1509 as part of a new expedition funded by the Spanish crown. His name was Francisco Pizarro.

CHAPTER 2

FIRST YEARS IN THE NEW WORLD

In the first decade of the 16th century, Columbus fell out of favor with Ferdinand and Isabella. After he had spent three years on Hispaniola and acquired very little gold or silver, he had secured investment for a voyage in 1498, certain that he could find a western route to Asia. On that voyage, he sailed along the northern coast of South America, where present-day Venezuela is located. He found little about the thick rain forests that appealed to him, and returned to the settlement at Hispaniola. The settlement still faced a struggle to survive and to find the wealth that the crown demanded.

Columbus's failures caused him to begin to act strangely. Caught between his desire to establish trade routes and the view of most conquistadors that the land be conquered, he was soon relieved of command by Francisco de Bobadilla. After one final voyage that took him as far as the Isthmus of Panama, Columbus returned to Spain a broken man. He died nearly penniless in 1506 in Valladolid, Spain, and was buried in a small cemetery.

Although Columbus's attempt to find a short route to Asia was a failure, many Spaniards were still eager to cross the Atlantic in search of wealth and fame in the New World. Exploration companies were formed to invest in expeditions to the region. These expeditions first had to be approved by the crown, which claimed ownership of the lands both discovered and yet to be discovered. Once approval was granted for it, an expedition followed a pattern that combined commercial, military, and religious goals.

Private Armies

A company-sponsored expedition was usually headed by a leader, or captain, who had invested most of the funds to pay for the expedition. Generally, these captains were wealthy nobles or men who had held some position in government. The lower-ranked company officers were men who had invested some personal funds to buy ships, supplies, weapons, and animals such as horses, dogs, and livestock.

The employees—those who did the hard work that was needed to fight and to build settlements in the thick, steamy forests of the New World—had little connection with the royal army. Few had any actual military experience at all. Many were merchants, craftsmen, and farmers who supplied their own weapons, equipment, and food in return for a share of any wealth that was won. Almost all the men who signed on for the voyage to America were people from lower social classes in Spain who could never hope to move up in status because of Spanish society's strict boundaries. For an illiterate campesino such as Pizarro, for example, life in Spain offered no chance for wealth, power, or respect. The stories that came back from those who had been to the New World attracted him simply because he knew he would be free to use his iron will in any way he wished, and there were few rules to prevent him from taking wealth and power. Pizarro was glad to leave his native land for the New World, where he might conquer a kingdom of his own.

Because few conquistadors had military experience, any man who came from a military background had an advantage. This was true of Pizarro, who was 37 when he arrived in Hispaniola and had spent many years in the army. Those years of service made him into a determined leader and a brutal fighter. It was the only way to advance in the Spanish military. His years of service paid off when he became a leader of the soldiers hired by the company.

Because the main objective of the conquistadors was wealth rather than trade, they focused their search on one item: gold. On Hispaniola, where the main Spanish settlement was located, however, there was very little of the precious metal. In order to make any money, the land had to be used to raise cash crops for sale in Spain. That work was accomplished with the slave labor of the native peoples who were captured by the conquistadors.

The expedition that included Pizarro arrived at a time when several of the native groups on the huge island had joined forces to drive the Spaniards off Hispaniola. Pizarro's knowledge of military tactics was immediately put to use against the natives, who greatly outnumbered the Spaniards.

Military knowledge, however, was not crucial in a land where Spaniards had many advantages over the native population in war. The natives did not have the technology to forge iron and steel as the Spaniards did.

The Spanish used primitive guns, crossbows, and war dogs against Native Americans.

Their main weapon, poison arrows, could not even penetrate the Spanish soldiers' breastplate armor. The natives had no knowledge of gunpowder, either. Although the Spanish guns were primitive, the sound was frightening, and even early guns such as the harquebus allowed the Spaniards to kill from a distance.

The Spaniards also had two fearsome animals that the Indians had never encountered. One was the horse, which was not only huge but gave the conquistadors an advantage in height and speed. The other was the mastiff war dog—a huge beast that stood almost four feet tall and weighed between 150 and 200 pounds. Pizarro executed natives by having them torn apart by his dogs. Against steel, guns, horses, and dogs, the natives were often overwhelmed.

The Spaniards also employed two strategies throughout their conquests in the first half of the 16th century. First, they took advantage of local rivalries to persuade weaker groups to help them destroy stronger groups. Second, they kidnapped the local chiefs and held them until a ransom was paid or until the chief's people surrendered.

Treatment of conquered natives was ruthless—often more brutal than the treatment of nonbelievers by the Inquisition. It was so harsh, in fact, that the plan to use natives as slaves often failed due to their high death rate. By 1516, 10 years after Columbus's death, all the islands in the Caribbean Sea had been explored by conquistadors. Many were under Spanish control. Thousands of natives had been captured on those islands and brought to Hispaniola to replace the thousands who had died.

From Panama to the Sea

By the end of the first decade of the 16th century, Hispaniola's small resources of gold and silver had already been mined. After shares had been sent to the Spanish crown and taken by the captains, there was little wealth left to be divided among the conquistadors. So little was mined there that later exploration companies turned their attention west to try to find greater wealth. Pizarro was among the conquistadors who left Hispaniola in search of gold along the coast of South America. His goal was to gain wealth or die in the attempt. There was no turning back. Once an area was shown to offer little gold, Pizarro moved on to another location.

In 1510, Pizarro served as second in command to Captain Alonso de Ojeda on a voyage along the coast of modern-day Venezuela and Colombia. The expedition came ashore and founded the settlement of San

Sebastian in Colombia. Within a year, intense heat, poison arrows, unclean water, and disease had killed hundreds of Spaniards. Ojeda was forced to return to Hispaniola for more men and supplies. He sailed back to Hispaniola and left Pizarro in charge.

As the death toll mounted, Pizarro became convinced that San Sebastian was not worth the many lives it cost to hold. With only one ship left behind by Ojeda, he waited until enough men died to allow the single remaining ship to sail away without sinking. Leaving the dead and dying behind, Pizarro sailed with the survivors back to a larger settlement along the coast. There, he joined forces

Pizarro served under Alonso de Ojeda (pictured) during a voyage to the coast of South America.

with Martín Fernández de Enciso, who had just arrived with a shipload of supplies for San Sebastian. Although he did not know it, Enciso was also carrying a stowaway, who revealed his presence when the ship docked. His name was Vasco Nuñez de Balboa.

Like Pizarro, Balboa had come to the New World in the early 1500s to seek his fortune. Balboa, however, had fallen deeply in debt. When he tried to leave Hispaniola to join an expedition and repay the debt, the men to whom he owed money prevented him. He was forced to stow away to escape from the island and seek his fortune elsewhere.

Pizarro was reluctant to return to San Sebastian, but Enciso convinced him to sail back. The ship set sail, and Balboa quickly began to assert his commanding personality. When they arrived in San Sebastian, the Spaniards found the settlement completely wiped out. Balboa told the others that the natives to the north, along the coast of Panama, were said to be relatively peaceful. He suggested that they sail there and establish a new settlement. In 1511, Pizarro, Enciso, and Balboa landed near the Isthmus of Panama and established the settlement of Darien, which became the first permanent European settlement on the continents of North and South America.

Balboa soon asserted control over the other conquistadors as well as the natives of the area. He convinced Pizarro and the other conquistadors to reject the leadership of Enciso, who left the settlement soon after Balboa took control. Pizarro, who realized that his

FRANCISCO PIZARRO

chance for wealth was greater with Balboa, became the chief military officer in any battles with native groups that refuse to submit to Spanish rule. As he had in Hispaniola, Pizarro used war dogs, guns, and horses to put down any resistance by native groups in the area around Darien.

When he returned to Spain, Enciso informed King Ferdinand of Balboa's actions. The king sent his own appointed governor, Diego de Nicuesa, to Darien. De Nicuesa was turned away by Balboa and Pizarro. On the way back to Spain, Nicuesa's ship sank in a storm, and the Spanish king held Balboa responsible for the death.

Unaware that the ship had sunk and ignoring the fact that he had not been given the title by the crown, Balboa claimed to be governor of Darien. He made trade treaties with local native groups and married the daughter of a local chief to solidify relations. Although Pizarro knew that without royal approval he would not be able to search for gold in the new region, he felt certain that Balboa would be accepted as governor and gain the approval needed. Throughout this time, Pizarro served as second in command to Balboa, as he done with Ojeda.

Over the next two years, Balboa developed and expanded good relations with the natives. As he did, he became curious about the stories that he heard from different native groups along the Caribbean coast of Panama. They said that another ocean lay across the narrow strip of land that formed the isthmus on which Darien was located.

Pizarro was intrigued by the idea of another ocean, but he found other stories from the natives even more interesting. These were tales of a powerful empire farther south, on the coast of an ocean that lay across the isthmus. There, Pizarro was told, gold was as common as iron was to the Spanish. The people there drank from golden goblets, said the natives, and ate from golden plates.

In 1513, Balboa set off with Pizarro and a party of more than 200 Spaniards and natives to locate and claim the western ocean for the crown. He believed that such an achievement would help persuade Ferdinand to grant him an official commission as governor, despite his earlier actions. The thick, tropical rain forest and steep hills made the journey extremely difficult. It took the party four weeks to cut its way through 45 miles of vegetation.

Despite these difficulties, the men persevered, and on September 29, 1513, Balboa waded into the waves of an ocean he named the Sea of the South—known today as

Balboa claimed the Sea of the South and its coastline for Spain.

the Pacific Ocean. He claimed the enormous body of water and all the coasts it touched for Spain.

While they rested and prepared to return to Darien, the Spaniards met with the leaders of several native groups in the region. Balboa was given a large amount of gold and pearls as tribute from the chiefs, a sign of respect from the natives who had never seen men with white skin and beards before. The tribute was so large that Balboa decided to explore the newly discovered region for other riches. This exploration took the party far from its original path. Balboa did not returned to Darien until the beginning of 1514.

Along with the news of the discovery of a coastline previously unknown to Europeans, Balboa sent gold and pearls to the king. He believed that he had done enough to earn the position he had already claimed. Unfortunately for Balboa, his news did not reach Spain until after the king—furious about Balboa's earlier disobedience—had named another governor for Darien.

In late 1514, a Spanish noble, Pedrarias de Ávila, arrived to govern Darien. Balboa was made second in command, and Pizarro was moved down to a lower position. Balboa did not object to his treatment, and continued with his plans to build ships in Darien and transport them overland to explore the Sea of the South.

Neither Ávila nor Pizarro, however, liked the division of power. Ávila resented Balboa's independent spirit and his popularity with both the conquistadors and with the natives. Pizarro, whose main loyalty was to his own success in finding gold, was caught between desire to follow Balboa and his realization that Ávila—who was backed by the king—had greater power. He knew that without royal approval, there was no chance that he would be able to claim the kingdom of gold to the south. Since his desire for gold outweighed any sense of loyalty, Pizarro began to seek the favor of Ávila. He recounted to Ávila the way that Balboa had turned away de Nicuesa in direct disobedience to the king, while absolving himself of any part in Balboa's actions.

Over the next several years, while Balboa and his men labored to build and transport ships, Ávila plotted against him with Pizarro's assistance. In 1518, Pizarro's subtle maneuvering earned him a position as second in command from Ávila. The governor then sent Pizarro to arrest Balboa on a charge of treason. The charge was weak, since it stemmed largely from Balboa's failure to obtain government permission for any of his explorations. Nevertheless, soon after Pizarro arrested Balboa, a show trial took place in the prison where Balboa was held. The result was predetermined by Ávila, and in 1519,

Cortéz and the Aztecs

Less than one month after Balboa was beheaded, the greatest Native American empire of Central America was entering its final years. Though the Aztec people of Mexico did not know it at the time, the landing of 400 Spanish foot soldiers, 16 horsemen, and a few cannons in February 1519 meant that their empire was under attack. This small force, which landed on Mexico's Yucatán peninsula, was commanded by Hernan Cortés. Cortés did not come to the new land to explore, trade, or convert non-Christians. He came for complete conquest and unlimited wealth. To prove his determination, Cortés ordered the ships that had brought his party to Mexico from Cuba to be burned in the harbor. There would be no turning back.

To conquer an empire with a population estimated at 12 million people with a little more than 400 men, Cortés used strategies that had succeeded for the Spaniards elsewhere in the New World. Following the advice of two native guides and translators, he formed alliances with small native groups that hated Aztec rule. By the time he reached the Aztec capital of Tenochtitlán in May 1519, Cortés had a large force made up of both Spaniards and native soldiers.

The Spanish conquest was also helped by an Aztec myth that predicted the arrival of a white-skinned god from the east. When they saw the Spaniards, especially the men who rode horses, which were unknown to them, the Aztecs welcomed the Spanish with gifts. When representatives of the Aztec king, Montezuma, approached, Cortés told them, "I and my companions suffer from a disease of the heart that can be cured only with gold." The warm welcome faded quickly, however, when Cortés employed a second successful strategy. He kidnapped Montezuma and held the king for ransom.

Although the Spaniards received a great deal of gold, Montezuma died as a prisoner. Enraged Aztecs forced the Spaniards out of the capital. Cortés, in return, laid siege to the city in 1521. By that time, a smallpox epidemic had struck the Aztecs. The disease was carried by the Spaniards, and with no immunity to the virus, the natives died in enormous numbers. The great capital fell, and Cortés claimed the largest single territory ever claimed by a European power until Pizarro.

Cortés became rich beyond his wildest dreams and made the Spanish king, Charles V, the wealthiest ruler in the world. The defeat of the Aztec empire was due more to disease than to military skill, and the diseases carried by

Cortés used the natives of Mexico to help conquer the Aztecs.

Europeans did not spare the native Americans who had helped Cortés. By 1550, the native population of Mexico had fallen to 3.5 million. An estimated 10 million natives had died in slightly over 25 years since Cortés's conquest.

Balboa and three of his closest followers were beheaded and their heads impaled on poles in the public square.

Pizarro soon became more than Ávila's second in command. He took charge of the exploration of the South American coast. His search for the kingdom of gold had begun.

CHAPTER 3

A DECADE OF JOURNEYS

By 1522, news of the conquest of the Aztecs—and of that empire's vast wealth—had spread throughout the Caribbean and reached Pizarro. A conquistador named Hernán Cortés had led a small force of just 400 men, 16 horses, and 10 cannons, against the Aztecs. The horses, which the natives had never seen, and the cannons, which killed from a great distance, made the Spaniards seem like the fulfillment of a religious prediction among the Aztecs. Cortés took Montezuma, the Aztec's chief, prisoner and held him for ransom. When the chief died, Cortés laid siege to the capital and tortured several of the Aztec religious leaders until they revealed the location of the king's treasury. The enormous amount of gold and silver that was sent back to Spain was the first indication of the wealth that the New World held.

Pizarro had spent the three years since Balboa's death in minor battles and conquests of tribes in Panama. When the news of the success of Cortéz reached Darien, many men left and headed north to join the hunt for treasure in the broken empire. Pizarro, however, did not want to go in a direction that had already been explored and where wealth had to be widely shared. He felt that his only opportunity for success would be to search for the kingdom of gold to the south. He had been in the New World for 10 years, and he was familiar with people who could help him figure out the steps he needed to take to achieve his goal.

Pizarro's first step was to obtain Ávila's permission to set off on a voyage to the south. Pizarro wanted to avoid the trouble that had caused Balboa's arrest and execution. To gain permission, he repeated to Ávila many of the stories he had heard of the kingdom of gold to the south. He promised Ávila a share of any riches he took.

Pizarro then sought out partners for his plan. His first partner was Diego de Almagro, a fellow conquistador, who, like Pizarro, had fought for many years against the natives. Almagro was considered one of the toughest and cruelest conquistadors. His job was to assemble the men and equipment for the voyage.

Pizarro then sought out a member of the Catholic Church—Father Hernando de Luque—as a partner. This partnership had less to do with Pizarro's religious beliefs than with the fact that Luque was literate and well read in Spanish law. Luque was also a man who understood that it was important to please people in the government with bribes and other favors. His role in the partnership was to stay in Darien and spy on the governor for Pizarro and Almagro.

Pizarro next had to find a way to finance his voyage. As news of Cortés's conquest of the Aztecs spread rapidly, many expeditions in the region were financed to travel north. To find financial support for a journey to unknown lands in the south was difficult and took Pizarro more than a year. Yet he refused to be denied an opportunity for wealth and power.

Finally, a wealthy settler named Gaspar de Espinoza agreed to finance the company. Not only did Espinoza agree to back the expedition, he also agreed to buy the

Pizarro (left) and Almagro (right) had spent years in the New World in search of wealth.

exploration rights to the South American coast. Earlier, Ferdinand had granted a Spanish noble permission to explore the region. That noble had not assembled an expedition, so Espinoza paid him for the right to finance an expedition to the area in which Pizarro hoped to find gold.

By 1524, Pizarro was the captain of a company called Empreza de Levante—The East Wind Company—and was prepared to set out to unknown lands south of Panama along the Pacific coast. A number of settlers in Darien, however, had another name for this expedition—Empresa de Locamentos—company of lunatics. These settlers believed that the only real wealth lay to the north, and that traveling to unknown lands was a foolish risk. For Pizarro, no risk was too great. At more than 50 years old, he was finally in command of an expedition that could bring him great wealth.

First Voyage

The first voyage of the East Wind Company set off in November 1524. Pizarro commanded one ship that carried 114 men and four horses. In the rush to begin the expedition, Pizarro left before a smaller ship commanded by Almagro was ready. Plans were made for the two to meet at a landing spot, several hundred

43

miles south along the coast of Colombia. Pizarro's ship sailed as far south as the San Juan River, which today forms the boundary between Colombia and Ecuador.

The Spaniards were attacked almost immediately by local natives. Nevertheless, Pizarro refused to turn back. He forced his men to fight their way inland through muddy mangrove swamps wearing their armor and thick cotton clothes. The march became nightmarish as the steamy dampness rotted the Spaniards' leather boots. Many of the men fell ill and died after they drank unclean water. As in San Sebastian, poison arrows and diseases carried by insects also killed many Spaniards.

At several points, they came upon native villages that had been deserted when word of the strangers' presence has passed among the people. Pizarro helped himself to whatever gold and other valuables he found in the empty villages. Although Pizarro was able to steal a small amount of gold from natives, he lost more than half his force—too many men to continue the march. He was forced to return to the coast and sail north to the small Spanish settlement of Chicama on the Pacific coast of Panama.

Meanwhile, Almagro had set sail with his smaller ship. His plan was to join Pizarro at the San Juan River and push inland. By the time he arrived, however,

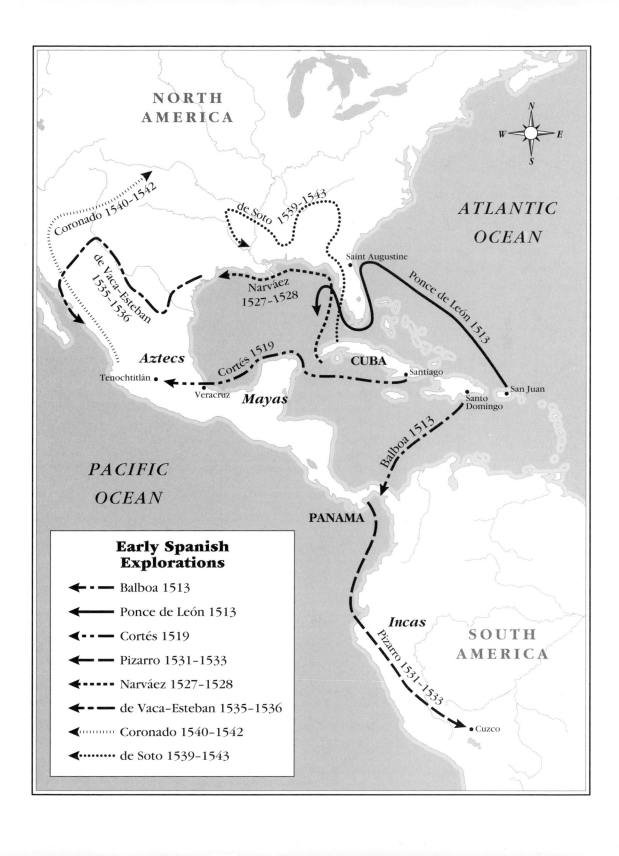

Pizarro had already left. Almagro and his men were attacked as Pizarro had been. Almagro lost an eye in a brief skirmish with natives. Wounded and unable to continue the expedition with his small force, Almagro sailed north until he found Pizarro at Chicama.

By this point, Pizarro had sent some of his men back to Darien with the gold he had taken. He hoped that this small amount would convince the governor and the company's backers to send reinforcements and funds for a second attempt. The first voyage's failure, however, raised doubts about the existence of a wealthy kingdom to the south—and about Pizarro's leadership abilities. Even Almagro began to question his partner's belief.

Second Voyage

Doubts about the possibility of success for Pizarro's partnership made Espinoza reluctant to fund another voyage right away. It took Pizarro and his partners several years to convince Espinoza to back another expedition to the south. Again, it was Pizarro's un-shakable belief that a huge kingdom of gold lay to the south that wore down the resistance of doubters who had money to back the expedition. Yet it also proved difficult for Pizarro to raise a force of conquistadors because most available men wanted to travel north to

Mexico, which was now under Spanish control. Pizarro used his powers of persuasion on these men as well.

Ávila withdrew his permission for the journey because he himself planned to lead an expedition north to an area in present-day Nicaragua. To do this, however, he had to resign his position as governor. Pizarro was forced to postpone his voyage until the newly appointed governor, Pedro de los Rios, arrived from Spain and reluctantly gave his permission to the East Wind Company to attempt another expedition.

Pizarro's second voyage set out from Panama's Pacific coast in 1526. This time, two ships sailed together, one under Pizarro and one under Almagro. Again the expedition landed at the San Juan River. Pizarro sent one ship under his experienced pilot and mapmaker, Bartolomeo Ruiz, farther south with orders to find landing sites and then return. He sent the other ship back with Almagro to Panama to bring reinforcements.

While Pizarro and his party pushed inland, the ship that sailed south under Ruiz encountered a huge native trading raft made of balsa wood—a material unknown to the Spaniards. Ruiz learned that the raft had sailed from a city called Tumbez on the coast of northern Peru. He was astonished by textiles made of the softest wool he had ever seen. The wool, along with a cargo of

47

gold, silver, and rubies, convinced Ruiz that there truly was a wealthy empire to the south. He headed back north to share his discovery with Pizarro.

Again, however, the Spaniards on land had suffered terrible losses from disease and native attacks. To escape the poison arrows of the coastal natives, they had built rafts and paddled to an island offshore to await Ruiz's return and reinforcements from Almagro. Eventually, what was left of the original force was reunited with men brought back by Almagro. Pizarro's partner informed him that the governor was furious that the company had nothing to show for its efforts. Pizarro's failure made the governor feel as though he had been foolish to send men on a wild chase to the south instead of sending them north where the promise of gold was almost assured. De los Rios had told Almagro that he would allow the expedition to be reinforced only under the condition that Pizarro himself return within six months.

Already in his late fifties, Pizarro knew that time was growing short for his success. For him, returning to Panama was not an option. He would find gold or he would die in the attempt. He drew a line in the sand with his sword. Pointing south, he exclaimed. "There [in the unknown land of Peru] lies toil, famine, nakedness,

48

rainstorms, foresakenness and death. Let he who will risk [desires] . . . riches, follow me; let he who will not, return [north] to . . . poverty."

Only 13 men stepped across the line to join Pizarro. After he sent the rest of the party back, he sailed to the city of Tumbez. There, finally, he found the empire of the Incas.

The Incas offered a warm welcome to the "bearded men," and held a banquet in their honor. The Incas proudly showed the wide-eyed Spaniards their gold and the silversmiths who created beautiful works of art. In return, the Spaniards showed the Incas how to fire their harquebus guns. The "thunder stick" convinced the Incas that these pale men had special powers that were rivaled only by their divine ruler, the Inca king himself.

Pizarro refused to give up his search for gold.

49

After they enjoyed the Inca hospitality, Pizarro and his men set sail for Panama with some "Inca sheep"— llamas—as well as a chest of golden trinkets and other items they had been given as gifts. On the voyage north, the Spaniards encountered another large balsa raft. This time they captured the vessel. A passage written by one of the Spaniards on the voyage described Pizarro's complete disregard for other lives, when they took control of the natives on the raft, which "carried twenty persons on board." According to the writer, Pizarro "threw eleven overboard. Of the others . . . three . . . were kept as interpreters . . . and were brought back with them."

Pizarro returned to Panama after a voyage of 18 months. With evidence of the existence of the fabled empire, Pizarro hoped to return south as soon as he could outfit another expedition. The governor, however, was not as enthusiastic as the partners of East Wind Company and refused any more support or funds.

By that point, Almagro and Luque had become as determined as Pizarro to conquer the Incas. Impatient to gain funds for a third voyage, they insisted that Pizarro take the evidence of the Inca empire directly to Spain. There he could seek support from King Charles V, Ferdinand's grandson, who now ruled Spain.

In June 1529, Pizarro arrived at the Spanish capital, then in the city of Toledo. It had been nearly 20 years since he had left his homeland. He had spent much of his adult life in the New World, with little to show for his years of work to help colonize Spain's empire.

Pizarro appeared at the royal court with Inca pottery, fine clothing, embroideries, and pieces of gold jewelry. After hearing Pizarro's story of his journey to Tumbez, Charles had no doubt that a wealthy empire lay on the Pacific coast of South America.

The Native Americans of the Pacific coast of South America had never seen men with beards who wore armor.

The king was also impressed by Pizarro's story of his line in the sand challenge, and his refusal to give up his quest despite terrible obstacles. Charles, a man under age 30 who had ruled for only a few years, had met few conquistadors as determined as Pizarro. Not only did Charles agree to invest in a third voyage, but he also made Pizarro a knight of the Spanish empire. Along with this honor, Pizarro was named a captain general in the Spanish military. Charles then granted Pizarro a license "to discover and conquer Peru . . . a rich and fertile land."

The grant named Pizarro a governor, with the right to explore and exploit Peru on behalf of the Spanish crown. As governor, Pizarro would have the power to choose government officials and to exert total control over the judicial system. In addition, he was to be paid a salary that was more money than he had earned in 20 years in the New World. Finally, the king sent Pizarro back to Panama in command of 250 soldiers with supplies to support the expedition.

A conquistador who served with him wrote that Pizarro was "as proud as he was poor and as lacking in rank as he was desirous of gaining it." After he appeared before Charles, Pizarro had achieved the greatest success of his life. Once he had tasted power, he began to desire it as much as he did the gold that always seemed just beyond his reach. He eagerly recruited men and gathered supplies for his return to claim the land he now considered his own.

Before he left Spain, however, Pizarro contacted his half brothers, whom he had not seen for 20 years. He offered his siblings, Hernando, Juan, Martín de Alcántara, and Gonzalo, an opportunity to share in his conquest and in his rule. In January 1530, Pizarro and his brothers set sail to rejoin the partners of East Wind Company, which was now solidly backed by the king of Spain.

By the time Pizarro returned to Panama, Luque had died of disease. Almagro was extremely unhappy when he learned of his partner's success in Spain. They were supposed to be equals, yet he had gained no title, a small salary, and little recognition for his part in the venture. Nevertheless, he now realized that his only chance of success was to follow Pizarro's orders, no matter how much of a dictator his partner had become.

Early in 1531, now almost 60, Pizarro set sail for Tumbez in three small ships with 180 men and 37 horses. With the title to the land given to him, Pizarro refused to consider any other option than complete conquest of the land that was now his. Almagro was left behind to recruit more volunteers from the few remaining men who had not gone to Mexico.

CHAPTER 4

SWEAT AND TEARS

Although Pizarro knew that the Inca kingdom was a land of great wealth, there was much that he did not know about the empire, which was known by its people as "The Four Quarters of the World." At the time Pizarro set sail from Panama, the Inca empire was the largest empire in the world and the largest native kingdom ever formed in the Western Hemisphere.

Stretching for more 2,500 miles from Colombia to Chile, the Inca empire was many times larger than Spain. The emperor of the kingdom, called the Lord Inca, ruled over a population estimated at between 10 and 12 million people from more than 100 native groups.

The empire was linked together by an amazing feat of engineering. A 12,000-mile-long paved stone highway ran north and south along the Andes mountain range, and a second highway ran parallel to that high road along the Pacific coast. Paved branches that extended far to the east and the west connected the two main roads.

Information was carried between Inca cities by a series of runners called *chasquis*, who were easily able to run 50 miles a day in oxygen-thin altitudes of over 15,000 feet. Because the Inca language, Quechua, was not written, *chasquis* carried quipus—a system of knotted strings—to help them remember the messages they carried.

Quipus were also used to keep government records. The colored, knotted strings were used to measure population in various regions, and to keep track of troop sizes, crop yields, and the size of animal herds. String colors stood for the objects to be counted. Red strings signified the number of soldiers, and yellow strings measured corn crops. Each quipu was like an individual record book and could be understood only by someone who was trained to interpret it.

The Inca people worshiped the sun, and they believed that their ruler, the Lord Inca, was descended from the sun.

FRANCISCO PIZARRO

The Inca empire flourished in some of the most extreme climates on earth. Its western Pacific coast was a desert. The east was bordered by the Amazon rain forest. The majority of Inca land, however, was in the Andes, the second highest mountain range in the world. Daily life for most Incas took place at altitudes between 11,000 and 15,000 feet.

Despite these extremes, the Incas were able to grow a surplus of hearty and highly nutritious crops, such as maize (corn) and grains, on terraced mountainsides. They also grew more than 200 kinds of potatoes. In fact, potatoes were so important to the Incas that the way they measured time was based on how long it took to boil different kinds of potatoes.

The Incas' primary source of meat was the guinea pig. Livestock that survived at high altitudes, such as the llama and alpaca— which Pizarro called "Inca sheep"—provided meat and fiber for cloth. Llama wool was used for bags and ropes. The soft fur of the alpaca was used for clothing.

57

The Empire of the Sun

The Inca empire originated in the late 13th century when several native groups united to establish the city of Cuzco, in central Peru. These people expanded their hold on the region for two centuries under a series of kings who came to be called Lord Incas.

The first of the rulers, Manco Capac, claimed that he was a child of the sun god, who gave him a golden rod and told him to place it at the spot that would become the capital of the empire, Cuzco. Because of this legend, the Lord Inca and his extended family—which included multiple wives for the king—were worshiped as gods by all of the Inca people.

As the Inca empire expanded, cities with massive stone buildings and temples were built as far north as Ecuador and as far south as Chile. The skill of the Inca builders enabled them to build huge stone structures without cement, sometimes with stones that weighed 50 tons fit together so tightly that a knife blade could not slide between them. Like the roads and terraces, the Inca buildings were built to withstand the harsh conditions of the Andes environment.

Inca society was as strictly divided as that of most European countries, if not more so, because the members of the nobility and royalty were considered

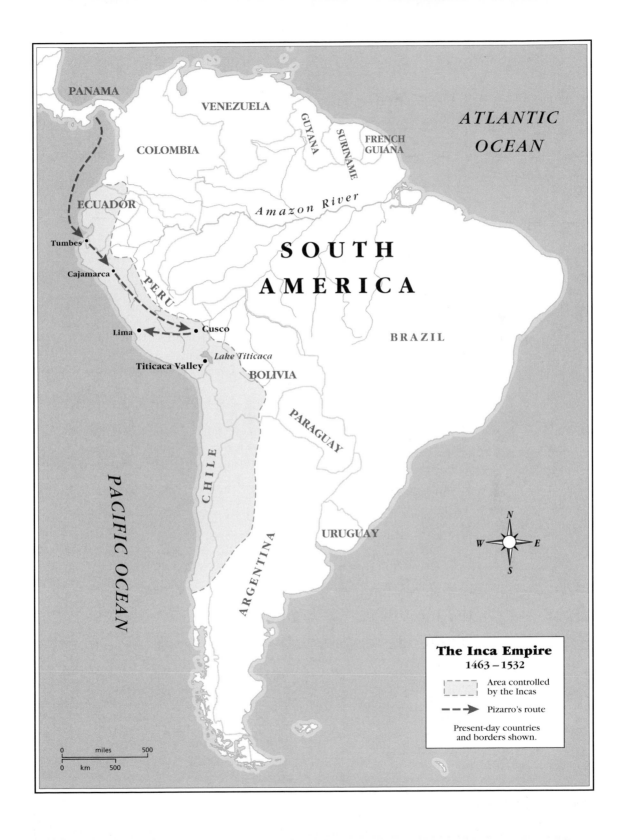

PANAMA

VENEZUELA

ATLANTIC OCEAN

COLOMBIA

GUYANA

SURINAME

FRENCH GUIANA

ECUADOR

Amazon River

• Tumbes

• Cajamarca

PERU

SOUTH AMERICA

• Lima

• Cusco

BRAZIL

Titicaca Valley •

Lake Titicaca

BOLIVIA

PARAGUAY

PACIFIC OCEAN

CHILE

URUGUAY

ARGENTINA

N
W ● E
S

The Inca Empire
1463–1532

Area controlled
by the Incas

Pizarro's route

Present-day countries
and borders shown.

0 miles 500
0 km 500

This gold goblet made by Inca craftworkers is one of the few artifacts that was not melted down by the Spaniards.

divine. The common people, however, had better living conditions than the peasants of Pizarro's homeland.

Instead of paying taxes in the form of money, crops, or livestock, Inca men provided a period of labor, called a *mita*, for the empire every year. Women were required to weave one piece of clothing per year for the government supply houses. Families were allowed enough time to raise their own crops and meet other family needs before they had to work for the empire. To build and maintain roads, terraces, irrigation canals, and temples required more than one billion hours of labor a year. As a result, the Inca government had representatives in every part of the empire, who kept records on quipus of an individual's hours of public service.

Laborers were given clothing and food for their work, but there was no pay for the time spent away from their homes. Money was not part of the Inca economy as it was in European nations that used gold and silver as currency. Gold and silver, however, were both extremely important to the Inca culture. The location of the empire in the Andes meant that streams and rivers washed huge quantities of the two precious metals down the mountainsides. Incas called gold "the sweat of the sun." Silver was called "the tears of the moon." Inca craftsmen worked gold and silver into practical items for the nobility such as goblets and plates. The soft, shiny metals were also used for sculptures, masks, religious items, and other art objects of great beauty.

Disease and War

In 1513, when Balboa reached the Pacific Ocean, the Inca empire stretched from southern Colombia to northern Chile. Over the next decade or so, the empire continued to flourish under the rule of Lord Inca Huayna Capac. Then, suddenly, the empire faced a threat unlike any it had seen in its 300-year history.

In the 1520s a *chasqui* who carried the news of the white men sailing south, arrived in Cuzco carrying something else as well—the smallpox virus. As it had done throughout the New World, the dreaded disease swept over the Incas. Eventually, millions of the Inca people died from disease. No one—not even the divine Lord Inca—was safe. Huayna Capac died of smallpox in 1528. The son whom he had named his heir to the throne, Ninan Cuyoche, died in the epidemic before his father did.

As Huayna Capac lay near death, he gave his title to his son Huáscar. Inca custom did not demand that a king pass his title on to his oldest son. Instead, the Lord Inca chose the son who seemed best able to rule the empire. Huáscar was considered kinder and more religious than his younger brother, Atahualpa, who was the only other possible heir. Atahualpa was a fierce warrior who had fought many years beside his father.

When Huáscar took the throne in Cuzco, Atahualpa did not attend the coronation. Instead, he remained in the northern Inca city of Quito in Ecuador, and sent a party of nobles to Cuzco with gifts for Huáscar. The new Lord Inca, enraged that his brother had not come to Cuzco to honor him, ordered his guards to cut off the noses of Atahualpa's men. He warned that anyone who remained loyal to Atahualpa would be treated in the same manner.

A civil war soon broke out between the supporters of the two brothers. Although Huáscar had more men under his command in Cuzco, Atahualpa had more experienced military commanders under him in Quito. After several bloody years, Atahualpa's army surrounded Cuzco, and made Huáscar a prisoner in his own capital.

Over a period of about three years—during which time Pizarro traveled to Spain and back—more than 200,000 Incas died in the civil war. Countless others had died of smallpox, and the once mighty Inca empire had started to crumble before Pizarro even arrived on the South American coast.

Although his iron will was key to Pizarro's success, the three-year period of civil war played a large role in the Spanish conquest. Had he attempted to conquer the largest empire in the world during the preceding decade, there is little chance that even an army with guns and horses could have defeated an Inca force of several hundred thousand fighting in the forbidding terrain of the Andes. By 1531, however, infighting among Inca groups had weakened the defense of their empire to outside invasion. As a result, Pizarro was able to conquer an empire of millions with little more than 200 men.

CHAPTER 5

THE FALL OF THE INCAS

When Pizarro landed in the Bay of San Mateo in northern Ecuador in mid-1531, he was unaware of the changes that had taken place in the Inca empire since he had left Tumbez. Because he believed that he would need a huge army to conquer Peru, he sent his three boats back to Panama to pick up recruits. Pizarro's party then began a slow march south along the coast to avoid the main Inca cities. The Spaniards were able to conquer a small coastal settlement, Manta, and Pizarro sent back gold and jewels with a courier to convince more men to join him.

By late 1531, a force of 100 Spaniards caught up with Pizarro's party at the town of Guayaquil, Ecuador, across the bay of the same name that faced Tumbez in northern Peru. In command of the reinforcements was a conquistador named Hernando de Soto, who later explored the Mississippi River and much of the present-day southwestern United States in the mid–sixteenth century.

The Spaniards were shocked when they arrived in Tumbez to find it completely destroyed. The beautiful city that had welcomed Pizarro and provided a glimpse of the riches of the Inca empire had been burned to the ground in the civil war between Atahualpa and Huáscar. Pizarro also saw that the few Incas left in the city were dying of smallpox.

The Spaniards continued south from Tumbez along the coast. On the march, they saw towns in ashes and bodies swinging from trees. With Inca translators—the men Pizarro had captured on the raft in 1527—to help speak to natives along the way, the conquistadors learned about the civil war and about the epidemic that ravaged the natives.

By the summer of 1532, the Spaniards had arrived in the small coastal village of Piura. There, Pizarro decided to wait for any reinforcements that Almagro might send or bring himself.

De Soto was a ruthless conquistador and an experienced cavalry officer.

Meanwhile, with Cuzco surrounded and Huáscar a prisoner, Atahualpa was making his way south from Quito to take the throne and the title of Lord Inca. Throughout the journey, he received information about the "bearded men in silver suits [armor]" who had passed through Tumbez.

"Every day, every hour," *chasquis* brought messages to Atahualpa about the progress of the pale-skinned men. The Incas had never before seen horses. As they observed these four-legged creatures that ate corn— an Inca staple—the *chasquis* told Atahualpa that the bearded men had with them giant four-legged humans.

During the journey south, Atahualpa discussed with his commanders whether he should attack the Spaniards. The military leaders felt it was more important to wipe out any forces that supported Huáscar. Atahualpa agreed with his commanders. It seemed impossible that such a small force of men could defeat the Inca empire, which, even after disease and war, still had a population of millions.

Slaughter and Betrayal

By September 1532, Pizarro was convinced that reinforcements would never arrive, and the men under his command were eager to continue the quest for treasure. On September 24, Pizarro left Piura and headed inland toward Cuzco, with a force of 170 foot soldiers and 67 cavalrymen.

Almost as soon as they left the narrow coastal region, the Spaniards began to climb into the steep Andes mountains. The men, who had become accustomed to the humid coastal region, shivered in cold mountain passes 11,000 feet high. The lack of oxygen made them feel faint and nauseated. The paths were so steep and narrow that cavalrymen had to dismount and guide their horses over the rocky paths. Still, the Spaniards made it over the coastal mountains into the valleys of modern-day Peru without the loss of a single man or animal.

Atahualpa, meanwhile, had stopped at the temple of an oracle—a religious figure who predicted the future. The would-be Lord Inca was uncertain whether to continue his journey to Cuzco or to turn west and conquer the bearded men. He was also eager to see, and perhaps capture, the four-legged humans. Finally, the ruler wished to see if the strangers truly had sticks that threw out fire and lightning, which he had heard about after they had landed at Tumbez five years earlier.

The oracle performed his ceremony and grimly informed Atahualpa that he would soon meet a "bad end." This warning only enraged the ruler, who ordered the oracle beheaded. Atahualpa then made one of the most significant decisions in the history of the Inca empire. He ordered his party to turn west to meet the bearded men rather than continue on to Cuzco.

Atahualpa sent an advance party to the Spanish with gifts, along with a message that he would meet them in the walled Inca town of Cajamarca. Once the Spaniards were inside the town, Atahualpa planned to surround them. He ordered some of his force to advance quickly ahead to the town and order the people there to evacuate.

When Pizarro's men arrived in Cajamarca in November 1532, they found it completely empty. Inca troops watched as the Spaniards entered the walled central area. Atahualpa then sent one of his commanders to position his men in a narrow pass that would block the Spaniards' escape route to the coast. The rest of his Inca army set up camp outside of town.

While his men occupied empty homes around the town square, Pizarro sent a cavalry squad led by his brother Hernando and Hernando de Soto to the Inca camp to make arrangements for a meeting. Like Atahualpa, Pizarro was plotting an ambush, one that would trap the king.

When they arrived at the huge encampment, the Spaniards saw that the Incas were frightened of their

Atahualpa was carried into Cajamarca on a litter of gold to meet Father Valverde.

horses. They decided to remain on the animals rather than dismount. As Atahualpa stepped forward, de Soto galloped directly at the king, which made the Inca guards scramble in panic. De Soto's horse came so close to Atahualpa that its breath ruffled the tassels on the king's crown. The king did not move a muscle, but he became furious with the guards who had run away. He ordered them beheaded.

As a sign of welcome and respect, the Incas gave the Spaniards golden goblets filled with *chicha*—Inca corn beer. Because they feared that the liquid was poison, de Soto and Hernando Pizarro poured it at the king's feet, a deeply insulting gesture. Atahualpa did not allow his men to attack the Spaniards, however, because he was convinced that they would soon be his prisoners.

De Soto then invited Atahualpa to come to Cajamarca the following day to meet with their leader, Pizarro. Atahuallpa agreed, and the Spaniards galloped off, leaving the angry and insulted Incas behind.

That night, Spanish sentries looked out on the campfires of a force estimated at 30,000 Incas. Few believed that they could defeat so large an army, but Pizarro, now more than 60 years old, was determined to conquer the Inca empire or die in the attempt. To achieve his goal, he had decided on a bold plan, a plan that had been used 10 years earlier by Cortés. He would kidnap the king. "Make a fortress of your hearts," Pizarro told his men. "You have no other."

Late the next day, November 16, 1532, the Spaniards received word that Atahualpa was on his way to the gates of Cajamarca. Crowds of natives, who had returned to the city to catch a glimpse of the mighty Inca leader, packed into the town square. The Spaniards hid behind doorways, in alleys, and in any place that gave them a direct path to the square but kept them out of sight.

Pizarro sent Father Vincent de Valverde to meet Atahualpa, who came to the plaza carried on a golden litter by the largest and strongest Inca soldiers. As the Spaniards tensed to attack, the priest read a document from the king of Spain. As the document was translated for Atahualpa, he became furious. He questioned the priest's right to make such demands of the ruler of the Inca empire. During the dialogue that followed, Valverde gave his Bible to the king. As the Spaniards had done the day before with the *chicha* offering, the Lord Inca threw the Bible angrily to the ground.

Valverde retreated into the shadows, and the attack commenced. The square exploded with the blare of bugles and screams. Using crossbows and harquebuses, the Spaniards slaughtered natives who never knew what hit them. The cavalry then charged into the square, and impaled Incas on their lances. Panicked natives fell over one another in a futile attempt to escape.

While the cavalry under de Soto chased the Inca outside of the city gates, the foot soldiers walked among the dead, and killed any Inca that groaned or moved. By that time, the litter-carriers of the king had been slain and Atahualpa had been taken by Pizarro to a room that overlooked the town square. In the square, the Inca ruler saw 8,000 of his subjects lying dead.

The first part of Pizarro's plan had worked perfectly. Not a single Spaniard had been killed, and the only injury was a cut that Pizarro himself had suffered as he pulled the Inca king to safety. Atahualpa's huge army retreated into the mountains, uncertain about its course of action without the Lord Inca to lead them.

Atahualpa was deeply distressed by his army's defeat, but he was even more concerned about his capture. Although the Spanish gave him food and clothing and allowed family members to visit, Atahualpa knew that without his leadership, his army would not press on to conquer Cuzco. They might even join forces with Huáscar to fight the Spaniards. Atahualpa did not want to lose his throne to supporters of his brother while he was imprisoned.

The old drawing portrays Pizarro talking with an Inca noble. In truth, Pizarro ordered the attack from a hidden position.

Finally, Atahualpa came up with a plan that would take advantage of the Spanish greed for gold—a greed that mystified the Incas. To the Incas, the value of gold and silver was only that it could be shaped into useful items as well as decorative objects and works of art. Since gold and silver could not be eaten or worn, they were not part of the Inca economy. The Spaniards' desire for it seemed strange and uncivilized to the Incas.

That desire for gold would gain his release, Atahualpa believed. He also thought that if the Spaniards were given enough gold and silver, they would leave the Incas alone. That would leave him free to battle Huáscar.

Late in December 1532, Atahualpa requested that Pizarro come to his cell—a room that was 17 feet wide by 22 feet long. The Inca promised to fill the room once with gold and twice with silver to a height of eight feet in exchange for his freedom. An astonished Pizarro agreed, and the two men put their marks on a written agreement, though neither could read or write.

Soon, news of the ransom agreement went out to the region controlled by Atahualpa, mainly the area north of Cajamarca as far as Quito. The Lord Inca granted the Spaniards the right to travel anywhere within his kingdom. He ordered all Incas to give the Spaniards any gold and silver they requested. Soon, gold and silver

objects began to arrive at Cajamarca by the thousands—
priceless masks, sculptures, icons, and plates were soon
gathered in the large room. To fulfill his promise took
Atahualpa much of the first part of 1533. During that
time, he established friendly relations with Hernando
Pizarro, played chess with him, and learned some
Spanish.

During the first months of 1533, Pizarro's partner,
Almagro, finally arrived in Cajamarca with about 200
men as reinforcements. Relations between the two
partners became strained when Almagro saw the
enormous treasure that had flooded into the city as
ransom. He demanded that the wealth be divided
equally between his force and Pizarro's men. The
demand caused Pizarro's brother Hernando to take
an immediate dislike to Almagro. The two men barely
avoided fighting. Pizarro and his men—especially
Hernando—felt that the latecomers deserved much
less than a full share, since they had not been involved
in the capture of the Inca ruler. The dispute carried on
through the first half of 1533, and further widened the
split between the two partners.

After more than six months, Atahualpa's ransom
had been paid. In order to make the division of wealth
easier, Pizarro built nine forges and had all the gold and

MACHU PICCHU

Under Pizarro and the governors who followed, the Spanish not only conquered the Inca empire, but attempted to erase it from history. Pizarro's men tore down Inca temples to build churches, and later built Spanish cities over the ancient Inca sites. One important Inca location, however, escaped destruction. It is Machu Picchu, a small city located about 50 miles northwest of Cuzco.

Machu Picchu—which means "old peak" in the Inca language—is 10,000 feet high on a mountain, hidden from a river valley below by thick clouds. It was built in the early years of the Inca empire, around A.D. 1300. The site is five square miles with more than 150 houses, palaces, and temples built from granite blocks that were cut from the mountain with stone tools. Stone outcroppings in the mountain itself were also used in the construction, and water from crevices flows through indoor fountains. Terraces that lead up the hillside to Machu Picchu were used for planting potatoes and corn.

The city itself, however, was more than an Inca settlement. It was a sanctuary and place of worship for the Inca sun god. Inca priests and nobles climbed the 3,000-step stairway for the solstice and gathered around the most important object there, the *intihuatana*, a stone column whose name means "hitching post of the sun." Because the sun reached its low point on the horizon at the solstice, a priest symbolically tied the sun to the *intihuatana* to prevent it from disappearing. The Inca believed that those who touched their foreheads to the *intihuatana* stone would be able to communicate with the spirit world.

In the early 1500s, *intihuatanas* were a key part of all Inca temples. The conquistadors destroyed every one that they found because the stones were considered an insult to the Catholic faith. The stone at Machu Picchu, like the city itself, because of its remote location, survived Spanish destruction. It was not discovered until 1911, nearly 400 years after Pizarro's death.

Machu Picchu was used for religious ceremonies by the Incas for hundreds of years.

silver melted down into bars of metal called ingots. The final ransom came to about 13,000 pounds of gold and 26,000 pounds of silver—a value of more than $250 million in today's money.

Pizarro first set aside a share for the Spanish king and sent his brother Hernando back to Spain to present it to the court. Taking his brother out of the city would prevent any violence between Hernando and Almagro. Pizarro then decided that Almagro would get a full share, but his men would get less. He promised the newcomers an equal share of any treasure to be found in Cuzco.

After the division of the ransom, Pizarro and Almagro were wealthy beyond their wildest dreams. Each man received about $11 million. Almagro's men received the smallest amount, about $52,000 per person.

The one obligation that Pizarro did not honor was his promise to free Atahualpa. The Inca leader had seriously miscalculated when he thought that the payment of a large ransom would send the Spaniards away satisfied. Instead, it made them even greedier.

They reasoned that if such wealth could be assembled in a small town like Cajamarca, the Spaniards agreed the treasures of Cuzco must be beyond their imagination. Only Atahualpa stood in their way.

Pizarro was well aware that if he freed the king, Atahualpa would unite his forces against the Spaniards and keep them from entering Cuzco. Even worse for Atahualpa, during his imprisonment, some of his supporters had murdered Huáscar. Thus, Atahualpa was by rights the sole ruler of the Inca empire. Pizarro and Almagro feared that if they freed the king, he could unite his own and Huáscar's armies against them. The Spaniards were not about to take that chance. In a plot to rid themselves of this threat, in August 1533, they charged Atahualpa with several serious crimes, including the death of his brother.

On August 29, 1533, a trial was held with Pizarro and Almagro as judges. Atahualpa was given a chance to defend himself, but he realized that there was no escape for him now. The court quickly found him guilty and sentenced him to be burned alive at the stake that same evening.

Atahualpa, accompanied by guards as well as by Pizarro and Valverde, was led to the square in Cajamarca, the place where thousands of his people had been killed nearly a year before. When he saw the wood piled beneath the stake, the king begged for mercy. The Inca religion claimed that for any soul to go to the afterlife, the body had to be mummified. To be burned would force an Inca to wander as a lost spirit.

Atahualpa converted to Catholicism so that he would not be burned to death.

Valverde told the king that if he converted to Catholicism, he would be given mercy and allowed to die in another way. The king agreed and was baptized. A Spaniard recorded the events that followed:

> "[Pizarro ordered Atahualpa] fastened to a pole in the open space and strangled. This was done, and the body was left until the morning of the next day, when . . . it was interred. . . . Such was the end of this man, who . . . died with great fortitude, and without showing any feeling."

With Huáscar dead and Atahualpa executed, the Inca army was demoralized and leaderless. The Spaniards had a clear path to their next objective—Cuzco, the Inca capital.

CHAPTER 6

THE VIOLENT END

When Hernando Pizarro brought the Inca gold to Charles V, the Spanish king was so pleased that he expanded the land grant he had given to Pizarro. He also made Almagro the governor of Chile.

As news of the treasure in Peru spread through Spain, men signed up by the thousands to join expeditions to the Inca lands. Soon, Spaniards flooded into Peru. A conquistador from Guatemala, Diego de Alvarado, led an expedition to conquer Quito, Ecuador, the former capital of Atahualpa's kingdom. Within a decade, the lands that were once part of the Inca empire were given as *encomiendas*—land grants—to Spaniards who were allowed to enslave any natives who lived there.

Though both Pizarro and Almagro had been named as governors of enormous regions of land, neither man cared as much about the area he controlled as about the wealth it offered. Both set their eyes on Cuzco, several hundred miles southeast of Cajamarca.

The Spanish left Cajamarca in September 1533. Though the Spaniards had fewer than 400 men, along the march Pizarro sought out native groups that had been conquered by the Incas. He built alliances with these people in an effort to turn the countryside against the Incas who remained loyal to the empire. In several skirmishes along the road to Cuzco, Pizarro and his new allies defeated Atahualpa's forces.

As word spread through the empire that the Inca rulers were dead, the lands they had conquered began to fall apart. There were many areas still divided by the forces that had fought in the civil war, and battles broke out between embittered forces who blamed each other for the collapsing empire.

Because he knew the opposing sides of Incas might unite against him, Pizarro named a brother of Huáscar, Manco, as the new Inca ruler. He hoped this act would convince the Inca people that he planned to treat them fairly. He also wanted Manco to take command of Huáscar's forces and defeat the remaining army of Atahualpa.

The City of Gold

By the time the Spaniards arrived at the gates of Cuzco in 1533, there was no need to fight their way in. War and smallpox had weakened any defense the Incas might have made. Revolts in the countryside kept the Inca troops on both sides occupied. The city residents had no strength left to resist the invaders who brought horses, guns, and diseases. Pizarro rode alongside Manco, and entered Cuzco in November 1533, a year after the massacre in Cajamarca.

The Spaniards entered a city unlike any they had ever seen. They saw Cuzco as a real version of the legendary "El Dorado"—the city of gold. A Spaniard wrote to Charles V that Cuzco was "the greatest and the finest [city] ever seen in this country or anywhere in the Indies. We can assure Your Majesty that it is so beautiful and has such fine buildings that it would be remarkable even in Spain."

Even as Pizarro assured Manco that the Spanish meant the Incas no harm, the conquistadors began to loot the city. Much of Cuzco's gold was in tombs and temples, which the Spaniards completely destroyed. A Spaniard wrote, "Some . . . immediately began to dismantle the walls of the temple, which were of gold and silver; others to disinter the jewels and gold vases that were with the dead."

Inca tradition called for a king to be buried with all the gold and silver from his palace. Entirely new objects and artworks were then made for the next king. "The riches . . . gathered in the city of Cuzco . . . were amazing and incredible," a Spanish priest wrote in a report sent back to Spain. "For therein were many big gold houses and enormous palaces of dead kings with all the . . . treasure that each amassed in life . . . he who began to reign did not touch the . . . wealth of his predecessor but . . . built a new palace and acquired for himself silver and gold and all the rest."

Because the Inca kings were all buried in Cuzco, the tombs were like treasure chests to the conquistadors. The Spaniards soon amassed a fortune in gold and silver that was even greater than the ransom paid for Atahualpa. The king's tombs, however, were only part of the wealth that the Spaniards found. The homes of the nobility were as magnificent as the palaces and temples. A Spaniard with Pizarro described one noble's house:

"There was the figure of the sun, very large and made of gold, very ingeniously worked, and enriched with many precious stones. . . . They had also a garden, the clods [dirt] of which w[as] made of pieces of fine gold; and it was artificially sown with golden maize, the stalks, as well as the leaves and cobs, being of that metal. . . . Besides all this, they had more than twenty golden [llamas] with their lambs, and the shepherds with their slings and crooks to watch them, all made of the same metal. There was a great quantity of jars of gold and silver, set with emeralds; vases, pots, and all sorts of utensils, all of fine gold. . . . It seems to me that I have said enough to show what a grand place it was; so I shall not treat further of the silver work of the chaquira [beads], of the plumes of gold and other things, which, if I wrote down, I should not be believed."

Pizarro was not content for the Spanish simply to plunder the Inca wealth. He also ordered his men to erase the Inca culture from history, to assure that it could not rise again and overthrow the Spanish. The Spaniards tore down Inca palaces and temples and rebuilt the city of Cuzco in Spanish style. They forced the Catholic religion on the natives and destroyed anything that had significance for Incas, even the quipus with which the Incas kept records. The Spaniards also went to great lengths to destroy the nobility and the military classes of the Inca empire. Inca farmers were forbidden to grow the special corn and grains that had been used to feed the nobles and warriors, so that the nobles would be forced to eat food like the common people and lose their special status in the culture.

By 1535, the destruction of the Inca empire and culture had reached levels of violence that exceeded the wholesale destruction of cities and culture of the Aztecs. Waves of newly arrived Spaniards enslaved and robbed natives across Peru. In Cuzco, Pizarro's brother Gonzalo stole the wife of Manco and forced her to marry him. When Manco protested the abduction, conquistadors walked into his palace and took gold and silver objects from his chambers.

By that time, Pizarro had left Cuzco and established a new capital city, which he named Lima, on the ruins of an Inca settlement. When Pizarro refused to take any action against the abusive behavior of his men, Manco decided to lead an uprising against the Spaniards. In 1536, native chiefs, with Manco's approval, led a series of revolts that killed large numbers of conquistadors. The overwhelming strength of the Spanish by that time,

Burning at the stake was a common method of execution used for rebellious Incas.

however, allowed them to end the rebellion quickly and brutally.

After one series of battles outside Cuzco that led to a Spanish victory, Hernando Pizarro ordered his men to kill any native women they captured. This, he believed, would stop the Inca soldiers, since it would take away a valuable support. After another raid in which 200 Incas were captured, a Spaniard wrote, "The right hands were cut off all these men . . . they were then released so that they would go off . . . as a . . . warning to the rest."

While violence swirled around Cuzco, the Inca empire collapsed in more remote areas. Native groups. left their fields and flocks untended to revolt against Inca armies on their lands. By the mid-1530s, a famine, caused by untended fields and the Spanish refusal to allow Incas to grow their staple crops, had struck across much of Peru and Ecuador. Widespread starvation added to the death toll from disease, conquest, and revolt.

As Inca control collapsed, many natives came to Cuzco with gold, in hopes of winning Spanish favor and buying food for their family. Soon the city swam in gold and silver. There was so much, in fact, that it became almost worthless. A period of inflation caused the price of a bottle of wine to rise to $1,500. A horse was worth

$7,000. Because of the famine caused by Spanish policies that forbid the cultivation of certain corn, potatoes, and other food crops, a bag of grain was worth more than an ingot of gold.

The Partners Part Ways

Ever since Pizarro had returned from Spain in 1530, his relations with his partner Almagro had grown steadily worse. Almagro felt that Pizarro had taken more than his share of the gold and the glory that had resulted from both of their efforts. By the 1530s, the two men were enemies who cooperated only because they were both under the control of King Charles V.

In 1535, the same year that Pizarro had left the city for the coast to establish Lima, Almagro took a force of volunteers and native slaves and marched south into Chile, the unexplored land that the Spanish king had granted him. Cuzco was left in the hands of Manco and two of Pizarro's brothers, Hernando and Gonzalo.

While Pizarro established the new capital of Peru, Almagro and his force suffered through a disastrous expedition. The area of northern Chile into which they had marched was one of the hottest and driest regions of South America. Not only did few people live in the area, it offered no gold or silver.

Almagro was furious that he had been made governor of a region that was worthless compared to the fabulous wealth that Pizarro had been given. To make up for this slight, Almagro claimed the right to govern Chile from the city of Cuzco. He sent a message to Pizarro in which he explained that his seat of government would be in Cuzco, while Pizarro's would remain in Lima. Pizarro was infuriated and refused to agree the new arrangement.

The Great Rebellion

In Cuzco, however, events had gotten out of the control of Pizarro's brothers. In the spring of 1536, Manco received permission from Hernando Pizarro to leave Cuzco to officiate over some religious ceremonies in the mountains. In return, Manco promised to bring back a large gold statue as a gift for Hernando.

Once away from Cuzco and into the remote mountains, Manco assembled a force of 150,000 Incas for one last attempt to expel the Spaniards. By May 1536, the Incas had surrounded Cuzco, which was defended by a force of fewer than 200 Spaniards. The Incas attacked, and soon much of the city was in flames. The Incas' use of slingshots and arrows forced the Spaniards to retreat into several small buildings where they were trapped. Fierce battles broke out over the ensuing week, but the Spaniards held their position.

Eventually, the Spaniards decided that they had to attack a large stone fortress outside of Cuzco's walls that was a gathering place for the Inca fighters. A cavalry force, led by Juan Pizarro, burst from the city and attacked the fortress. He was killed in the attack, but the Spaniards eventually defeated the Incas. They executed more than 1,500 Incas and left their bodies for the vultures.

That victory diminished the morale of the Incas, but they still far outnumbered the Spaniards and had them surrounded. In Lima, Pizarro ordered cavalry units to Cuzco, but more than 200 Spaniards on horseback were killed in the steep mountain passes when Incas threw huge boulders down on them.

By the end of 1536, a stalemate had developed between the Spaniards in Cuzco and Manco outside the walls. Neither side knew that Pizarro had sent word of the Inca rebellion to Spanish colonies throughout the New World. Spanish soldiers were gathering in Lima to march to Cuzco.

Meanwhile, Almagro was near Cuzco on his return from Chile. When he saw that the Incas had the city surrounded, he took advantage of the opportunity to

Manco led the last rebellion against the Spaniards in Peru.

FRANCISCO PIZARRO

gain power over Pizarro. First, he ordered
his men to drive the Incas from around
Cuzco. Then he took command of the
city, and the Pizarro brothers became
his prisoners. Gonzalo escaped, and
Hernando was released as a gesture of
goodwill from Almagro, who hoped that
this act would persuade his longtime
partner to allow him to rule from Cuzco.

The two brothers joined Pizarro, who
was by then on the march from Lima
with a force of more than 500 men.
In April 1538, a battle between the
opposing forces of Almagro and Pizarro,
former partners in the East Wind
Company, took place on the plains
outside Cuzco. Pizarro's soldiers defeated
Almagro's men, and Almagro was taken
prisoner. In July 1538, on Pizarro's
orders, Diego Almagro was strangled
and then beheaded.

Over the next several years, despite
battles between Incas and Spaniards
throughout Peru, Francisco Pizarro
solidified his hold on power and became

97

one of the wealthiest men in the New World. After he established Lima, he founded another city farther up the coast and named it Trujillo, after the town of his birth.

Two of Pizarro's brothers, Martín and Juan, died from disease. Hernando Pizarro returned to Spain, where he was surprised to be charged with the murder of Almagro, the governor of Chile. Hernando died in a Spanish prison. Gonzalo Pizarro formed an expedition to explore eastern Peru, and became one of the first white men to venture into the Amazon rain forest.

The Incas and other native people continued to die in enormous numbers. As they had done in other areas of conquest, the Spaniards enslaved the natives. When the supply of gold diminished, silver mines were dug in the mountains. Hundreds of thousands of Inca died as they worked in the mines and on the huge farms that were established by wealthy Spanish immigrants who claimed vast regions of land under the *encomienda* system.

Although Pizarro was honored by Charles V as the greatest conquistador of the New World, he was thoroughly hated by a large number of Spaniards. These were the followers of Almagro, who felt that they had been cheated out of their fair share of the Inca treasures and believed their leader had been murdered.

In June 1541, Pizarro, now about 70, sat down to dinner in his private chambers at his palace in Lima. Suddenly, a group of more than 20 men who had overpowered the palace guards burst into the room. Although he was an old man, Pizarro remained a conquistador to the end. He grabbed a weapon and tried to fight off his attackers. The brief battle that followed was described by one of the attackers— Almagro's son, Diego:

> *"He placed himself in a doorway with a halbered and defended himself very well—so well that [we] could not enter, as it was a narrow door... [we] gave the Marquis [Pizarro] so many lance thrusts, stab wounds and sword slashes that he died."*

As he died, Pizarro cried out, "Jesus," and made a cross on the floor with his own blood. After his death, he was beheaded by his assassins. His remains were taken to the cathedral in Lima where they were interred.

Epilogue

After Pizarro's death, the followers of Almagro, led by his son, took control of Lima for a year. They were eventually driven out by Pizarro's supporters, led by

Pizarro was murdered by Almagro's followers.

Gonzalo Pizarro, who had returned from an expedition to the rain forest to learn of his brother's death.

Gonzalo Pizarro then led a revolt of Spanish landholders whose *encomienda* rights were suddenly taken away by Charles V in the 1540s. The revolt failed, and Gonzalo was captured and beheaded by Spanish troops.

Manco continued to rule a small kingdom of Inca followers in an area north of Cuzco. In the 1540s, he was murdered by Spaniards. At that point, the rule of the Incas was passed down through Manco's four sons. Tupac Amaru, the last son—also known as the "Last Inca"—was beheaded by the Spaniards in 1572. The execution took place in the square of Cajamarca, the same place where Pizarro had ordered Atahualpa executed almost 40 years earlier.

In 1525, when the Inca empire was at its height of power under Huayna Capac, the population was estimated at about 12 million. By the time of Tupac Amaru's execution, the population of natives in the lands once ruled by the Inca was slightly over 3 million.

Historians have written that the conquistadors came to the New World for "God, gold, and glory." From the Spanish point of view, Pizarro was perhaps the most successful of all conquistadors. He conquered the largest empire in the world, subdued the population, and sent more gold to Spain than any other explorer.

An illiterate peasant, Pizarro realized that his only hope for a better future lay outside of Spain. He fought to achieve success by any means possible, even when that success meant the complete destruction of one of the most advanced cultures in the world at that time. He is estimated to have acquired a personal fortune of nearly $100 million in today's money. As for glory, there are many who would say that the destruction of the Inca empire was anything but glorious and honorable. To many people, Francisco Pizarro was one of the great villains in history.

TIMELINE

1471 Francisco Pizarro is born in Trujillo, Spain.

1478 Spanish Inquisition begins.

1492 Spain becomes a united country under Ferdinand and Isabella; Columbus lands in the Bahamas.

1493 Huayna Capac becomes Lord Inca and expands the Inca empire north to Colombia.

1509 Pizarro arrives in Hispaniola.

1510 Pizarro sails to the coast of South America under Ojeda.

1511 Pizarro establishes the colony of Darien with Balboa in Panama.

1513 Balboa crosses the Isthmus of Panama and sees the Pacific.

1519 Balboa is executed.

1522 Aztec empire falls to Cortés.

1524 Last Aztec ruler is hanged.

1524 Pizarro, Almagro, and Luque form a partnership and prepare to explore the Pacific coast of South America.

1524 Pizarro leads a voyage that becomes stuck in the swamps of Ecuador.

1527 Pizarro and 13 men land at Tumbez and are welcomed by Incas, which confirms the rumors of the existence of a wealthy kingdom.

1527   Lord Inca Huayna Capac dies of smallpox.

1528   Civil war for succession begins between Huáscar and Atahualpa.

1529   In Spain, Pizarro receives the support of King Charles V for an expedition to South America.

1531   Pizarro's third expedition occupies Tumbez.

1532   Atahualpa's forces surround Cuzco and Huáscar's forces; Atahualpa moves south with his court and army and camps near Cajamarca.

1532   **November 15:** Pizarro and his men camp in the plaza at Cajamarca; Hernando Pizarro invites Atahualpa for a meeting with Francisco Pizarro.

1532   **November 16:** Pizarro ambushes and captures Atahualpa at Cajamarca

1533   Huáscar murdered.

1533   **August 29:** Pizarro executes Atahualpa.

1533   **November:** Cuzco falls to Spaniards.

1538   Almagro killed by Pizarro's followers.

1541   Pizarro killed by Almagro's followers.

GLOSSARY

commerce trade in raw materials and goods

empire large territory usually ruled by a king or emperor

epidemic sudden widespread outbreak of disease

expedition journey undertaken for a specific reason

famine widespread starvation

harquebus early gun

isthmus a narrow strip of land separating two larger land areas

massacre killing a large number of defenseless people

peasant uneducated person of low social standing

ransom money demanded or paid for the release of a captive

siege military blockade of a fort or city

virus small organisms that cause disease

Source Notes

Introduction

Page 6: "I am a priest of God..." *Narrative of the Conquest of Peru*, by Francisco de Xeres 1530–1534 web site http://www.fll.vt.edu/culture-civ/spanish/texts/spainlatinamerica/pizarro.html

Chapter 1

Page 19: "distant lands to the west" *Christopher Columbus and the Spanish Empire* http://www.ucalgary.ca/applied_history/tutor/eurvoya/columbus.html

Chapter 3

Pages 48–49: "There...lies toil, famines, nakedness, rainstorms, forsakeness and death." *Incas and Conquistadors* Web site http://www.hc09.dial.pipex.com/incas/spanish-francisco.html

Page 50: "threw eleven overboard..." *History of the Conquest of Peru* by William Prescott Chapter 10. World Wide School Web site http://www.worldwideschool.org/library/books/hst/southamerican/HistoryoftheConquestofPeru/chap10.html

Page 52: "to discover and conquer..." *The Would-Be Conqueror* from Web site Inka Crops, North America http://www.inkacropsna.com/

Page 52: "as proud as he was poor..." ibid.

Chapter 4

Page 54: "The Four Quarters of the World." Peru: *Conquest of Paradise Web* site http://www.geocities.com/CapitolHill/6502/conquest.htm

Chapter 5

Page 67: "bearded men in silver suits." *Peru: Conquest of Paradise* Web site http://www.geocities.com/CapitolHill/6502/conquest.htm

Page 67: "Every day..." ibid.

Page 68: "bad end" *The Would-Be Conqueror* from Web site Inka Crops, North America http://www.inkacropsna.com

Page 83 "fastened to a pole in the open space and strangled." *Incas and Conquistadors* Web site http://www.hc09.dial.pipex.com/incas/spanish-francisco.html

Chapter 6

Page 86: "the greatest and finest..." *Incas and Conquistadors* Web site http://www.hc09.dial.pipex.com/incas/spanish-francisco.html

Page 87: Some ...immediately began to dismantle..." *Incas and Conquistadors* Web site http://www.hc09.dial.pipex.com/incas/spanish-francisco.html

Page 87: The riches...gathered in the city of Cuzco..." Ibid.

Page 88: There was a figure of the sun..." *Peru: Conquest of Paradise* Web site http://www.geocities.com/CapitolHill/6502/conquest.htm

Page 100: He placed himself in a doorway..." *Incas and Conquistadors* Web site http://www.hc09.dial.pipex.com/incas/spanish-francisco.html

FOR FURTHER READING

Bergen, Lara Ruce. *Travels of Francisco Pizarro*. Austin, TX: Raintree-Steck Vaughn, 2000

Deangelis, Gina. *Francisco Pizarro and the Conquest of the Inca*. Minneapolis, MN: Chelsea House Publications, 2000

Jacobs, William. *Pizarro: Conqueror of Peru*. Danbury, CT: Franklin Watts, 1994

Marrin, Albert. *Inca & Spaniard: Pizarro and the Conquest of Peru*. New York: Atheneum, 1989.

WEB SITES

The Inca Empire
http://www.inkacropsna.com/the_inca_empire.htm
Good historical and cultural resource.

Conquistadors: The Conquest of the Incas
http://www.pbs.org/conquistadors/pizarro/pizarro_flat.html
Good public broadcasting site with information about Atahualpa's
  capture.

Conquest of the Inca Empire: Francisco Pizarro
http://www.ucalgary.ca/applied_history/tutor/eurvoya/inca.html
Good site for overall look at Spanish conquest of the Americas.

Spaniard v. Incas and the Fall of the Inca Empire
http://muweb.millersville.edu/~columbus/papers/white.html
Offers historical background.

Incas and Conquistadors
http://www.hc09.dial.pipex.com/incas/conquest-1535.html#top
Excellent source for history of Inca rulers.

Index

Francisco Pizarro